HISTORY FROM OBJECTS

The Tudors

Angela Royston

WAYLAND

First published in 2010 by Wayland
Copyright © Wayland 2010
This paperback edition published in 2012 by Wayland
Wayland, 338 Euston Road, London NW1 3BH
Wayland, Level 17/207 Kent Street, Sydney, NSW 2000

British Library Cataloguing in Publication Data
Royston, Angela.
The Tudors. — (History from objects)
1. Material culture—England—History—16th century—
Juvenile literature. 2. Great Britain—History—Tudors,
1485-1603—Juvenile literature.
I. Title II. Series
942'.05-dc22

ISBN: 978 0 7502 6765 6

Produced for Wayland by Calcium
Design: Paul Myerscough
Editor: Sarah Eason
Editor for Wayland: Camilla Lloyd
Illustrations: Geoff Ward
Picture research: Maria Joannou
Consultant: John Malam
Printed in China

Pic credits: Alamy Images: Robert Harding Picture Library Ltd/Adam Woolfitt 17b; Corbis: Ho/Reuters 9b;
Fotolia: Petr Kratochvil 8; Shutterstock: Norma Cornes 11t, Alexander Orlov 12b, Stephen Aaron Rees 3, 20t,
Jane Rix 7t; The Picture Desk: Art Archive/Eileen Tweedy 7b; Wayland Picture Library: 4, 10, 11bl, 11br, 12t,
15b, 17t, 18b, 21b, 22, 23b, 26c, 27t, 27b; Wikimedia Commons: 9t, 13, 14, 16, 18t, 19b, 20b, 23t, 24, 26b,
Eric Brandwine 5, 15t, Davepape 19t, Pierre Dunand Filliol 25t, M. S. Tea 25b, Myriam Thyes 21t, Zenodot
Verlagsgesellschaft mbH/The Yorck Project 6, 26t.

Cover photograph: Wayland Picture Library

Wayland is a division of Hachette Children's Books, an Hachette UK company.

www.hachette.co.uk

Contents

Who were the Tudors?

The Tudors were a family of kings and queens who ruled England and Wales between 1485 and 1603.

Wars of the Roses

Henry Tudor became King Henry VII when he defeated King Richard III in the Battle of Bosworth Field in 1485. This ended a civil war called the Wars of the Roses. During this war, two families, the houses of Lancaster and York, fought for the crown.

Strong and united

Tudor kings and queens wanted to make England strong. Henry VII, a Lancastrian, married Elizabeth of York and joined the houses of Lancaster and York. His son, Henry VIII, was desperate to have a son to rule after him. He thought that only a man could be a strong leader.

 Henry VIII ruled England from 1509 to 1547. He was a tall, heavy man who became a cruel king as he grew older.

Age of change

The 1500s were a time of great change in Europe. In Germany, Martin Luther disagreed with the **Roman Catholic** Church about some of its beliefs. Luther and his followers broke away from the Catholics and became **Protestants**.

> ### A SON AND HEIR
> Henry VIII married six wives in his wish for a son. This rhyme tells you what happened to each wife:
> Divorced, beheaded, died;
> Divorced, beheaded, survived.

At the same time, explorers were sailing the world's oceans and discovering great new continents. They brought back goods to sell at home and abroad. These changes affected the people of Tudor England. Their lives improved, and many people became richer.

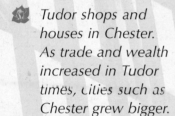 Tudor shops and houses in Chester. As trade and wealth increased in Tudor times, cities such as Chester grew bigger.

What does it tell us?

This drum belonged to Sir Francis Drake – he took it on many sea **voyages**. The drum was used to beat time as the crew carried out their tasks on board the ship. Drake also played the drum to entertain his crew. When he died, Drake said if England was ever in danger again, the drum would sound and he would return to fight once more!

The Tudors and religion

Most English people were Roman Catholics when the Tudors came to power. Henry VIII married Catherine of Aragon, a Spanish princess who was also a Catholic. Henry was religious, too.

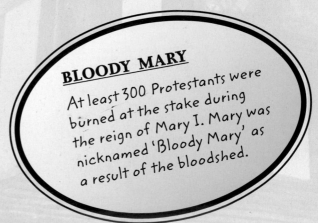

Fountains Abbey in Yorkshire is one of the many abbeys that Henry VIII ordered to be destroyed during his four-year Dissolution of the Monasteries.

Henry and religion

In 1521, Henry wrote a book defending the Roman Catholic Church from the Protestants. As a result, the **Pope**, the head of the Roman Catholic Church, gave him the title 'Defender of the Faith'.

Henry had an argument with the Pope in 1526. Henry wanted to divorce Catherine because she had given him a daughter, Mary, but not a son. Catherine did not want a divorce, and the Pope took her side.

A new church

Henry left the Catholic Church and set up the Protestant Church of England. He then married Anne Boleyn. Henry destroyed **monasteries** and **abbeys** and stole their wealth. We know what happened from the accounts people wrote at the time.

BLOODY MARY

At least 300 Protestants were burned at the stake during the reign of Mary I. Mary was nicknamed 'Bloody Mary' as a result of the bloodshed.

Battle between religions

Religion was a dangerous business in Tudor times. Henry VIII was followed by his son Edward VI, who was a Protestant. He tried to force all Tudors to become Protestants. Edward died when he was young. His elder sister, Mary, became queen. Mary was a Catholic like her mother. Anyone who refused to become a Catholic was tied to a wooden stake and burned alive.

When Mary's younger sister, Elizabeth became queen in 1558, she restored the Protestant Church of England. Elizabeth was much less strict than her brother and sister. However, Catholics could only practise their religion in secret during her reign.

William Tyndale was the first person to translate the Bible into English. Protestants believed that people should read the Bible themselves in a language they understood.

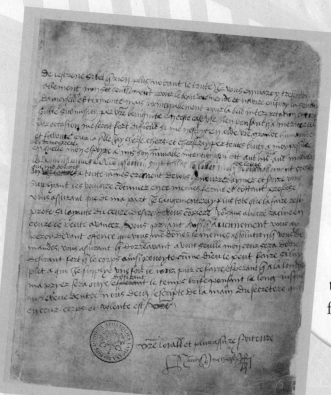

What does it tell us?

Henry VIII wrote many love letters to Anne Boleyn during their love affair. The letters tell us how Henry planned his future with Anne and intended to divorce his wife Catherine to make Anne queen. Henry's royal **seal** of the Tudor rose can be seen at the foot of this love letter.

Tudor homes

During the Tudor period, England became stronger and richer. Many people became wealthier, too, and lived in more comfortable homes.

Towns and cities

The **population** of England doubled in Tudor times. This led to the building of thousands of new houses in many English towns. Tudor buildings still stand in Chester, Stratford-upon-Avon, Norwich and other historic town and city centres.

Great houses

Many rich people built large houses in the countryside to show off their wealth. Many of these houses still stand. The **deeds** to the houses tell us who built them. For example, Kelmscott Manor in Oxfordshire was built by a farmer during the reign of Elizabeth I.

Tudor houses were built mainly of wood. Oak beams were used to make a frame, which was covered with wood and plaster. Wood burns easily, so the chimneys were built of bricks. Some large houses were built of bricks or stone.

This four-poster bed dates back to Tudor times. It is made of oak and has carved panels at each end.

What does it tell us?

This manor house has large, glass windows. Window glass for homes came into use in Tudor times, but it was difficult to make and was also very expensive. Large, glass windows let in light and showed people how rich the owners were.

Greater comfort

Huge fires heated the rooms of Tudor houses, and the walls were covered with oak panels and tapestries. Rich people put carpets on their floors. In 1589, Sir John Harrington installed the first water closet (toilet) in his home near Bath. Not all Tudor houses were comfortable, however. Poor families often huddled together in one or two dark and dingy rooms, with floors covered in **rushes**.

> *There was no gas or electricity in Tudor times. People had only candles (left) and fires (right) to light their homes at night.*

SMELLY FLOORS

Poor families covered their floors with rushes. They collected all kinds of spills and litter, including cat and dog droppings. They smelt terrible!

Food and drink

The Tudors loved food. Wealthy people entertained with huge **banquets**. Most people ate well compared with earlier times.

Meat eaters

People ate a wider range of meat than we do today. A wealthy family might eat mutton, chicken, duck and **woodcock** in one meal! Rich people ate few vegetables or dairy food such as milk and cheese. They thought that vegetables were poor people's food, even though we now know they are healthy. Poor people also ate thick soup or broth, rye bread and meat when they could afford it.

This Tudor kitchen is in Hampton Court Palace, one of Henry's many palaces. The food was cooked over fires in the huge fireplace.

What does it tell us?

This drinking vessel has been made from animal skin. It shows that wealthy Tudors hunted for pleasure as well as food. Henry VIII loved hunting and chased deer and other animals in his **royal parks**.

Banquets and feasts

Tudor kings and queens put on great banquets to impress **ambassadors** or foreign rulers. The banquet could last for seven hours and have ten courses or more. Many of the dishes were designed to amaze. Cooks stuffed peacocks and swans with smaller birds, such as pigeons. They even filled pies with live birds that flew out when they were cut open.

Growing food

People bought most food from weekly fairs and markets. However, many people kept a pig and had a garden to grow vegetables, such as onions, and herbs to add flavour to their food. New spices arrived from overseas and these were also used to flavour food.

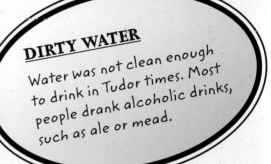

DIRTY WATER

Water was not clean enough to drink in Tudor times. Most people drank alcoholic drinks, such as ale or mead.

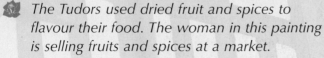 *The Tudors used dried fruit and spices to flavour their food. The woman in this painting is selling fruits and spices at a market.*

clothes

Working people wore hard-wearing clothes in Tudor times. Rich people dressed more grandly. The clothes of the king or queen were the most expensive and magnificent.

Dressed to impress

A person's clothes clearly showed how well-off and powerful he or she was. The most important people dressed in the finest, most expensive materials, such as silk and fine wool. There were even laws to tell people what they could and could not wear. For example, only the monarch could wear clothes trimmed with a soft white fur called **ermine**.

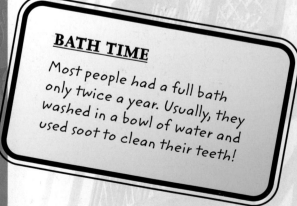

BATH TIME

Most people had a full bath only twice a year. Usually, they washed in a bowl of water and used soot to clean their teeth!

Children, such as the young girl in this painting, were dressed to look like small adults in Tudor times.

Women's clothes

Most of the time, women wore caps or hats. Their dresses usually had high collars. Wealthy women often wore a ruff. This was a thick, wide collar that fastened around the neck. Working women protected their dress with an apron. Women wore many petticoats under their dresses.

What does it tell us?

Men and women carried a pomander, such as the one shown to the right. This was a small container that held sweet-smelling herbs. The pomander helped to block out smells in the dirty Tudor streets. It also masked the wearer's bad smells as well as those of other people.

Men's clothes

When Henry VII became king, most men wore hose (tights) and a tunic called a doublet, which was padded around the hips. Working men wore a warm woollen jacket outside, while wealthy men wore a short robe or gown. By the time Elizabeth came to power, men wore breeches (trousers that finished just below the knee). Men also wore ruffs around their necks and wrists.

 The young man in this painting is wearing a doublet and hose. He also has a short cloak slung over his shoulder and a ruff around his neck.

Children and schools

Childhood did not last long in Tudor times. Many babies did not even survive because there was so much illness.

Little adults

Children who did survive were treated strictly and were expected to behave like adults. Children from poor families were sent out to work from about the age of eight. Girls could be married as young as 12 years old.

Schools

Many new grammar schools and public schools were built during Tudor times. School began at 6am and went on until 5pm, six days a week. Latin, Greek, ancient history, religion and English were the main subjects.

Only boys went to school. Tudor girls were expected to marry and have children, so parents thought there was little point in them going to school. However, private **tutors** often taught girls from wealthy Tudor families, alongside their brothers.

Children learned to read from hornbooks such as these. The words were printed on paper, mounted on a wooden frame and covered with transparent (see-through) animal horn.

WHIPPING BOYS

Wealthy boys often avoided being whipped by paying a 'whipping boy'. This was a poor boy who took the punishment instead.

Road to success

Education allowed boys from poor families to get good jobs. **Parish registers** record the jobs that parents did when a baby was **christened**. Thomas Wolsey, who held the highest office in the land under Henry VIII, was the son of a butcher. William Shakespeare, the greatest playwright in English history, was the son of a glove-maker.

This simple wooden carving may have been used as a doll.

What does it tell us?

This is a classroom at the Grammar School in Stratford-upon-Avon, where Shakespeare went to school. The room is large with lots of desks. This shows that classrooms would have been crowded with many pupils.

Castles and weapons

Weapons changed in Tudor England. Before this, in **medieval** times, men fought with swords and wore **armour**. The invention of **cannon** and **muskets** changed the way people fought.

Tudor warfare

Cannon fired cannonballs that could knock down the walls that protected medieval castles. By the end of the Tudor period, knights carried muskets as well as swords to defend themselves.

A musket was propped on a stick to steady the firer's arm.

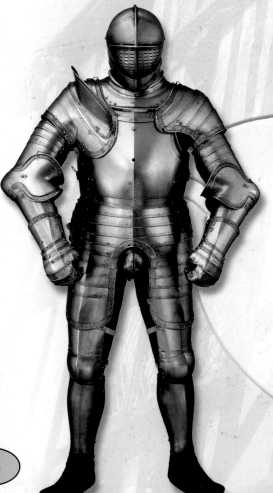

What does it tell us?

This suit of armour belonged to Henry VIII. It shows what a big man he was. Henry had a full set of armour because he loved to **joust** in tournaments. A tournament was a mock battle in which **chivalrous** knights on horseback charged at each other and tried to knock each other to the ground with a long lance.

Castles

Henry VIII built a chain of strong, round castles along the south coast of England. Many of these castles still exist. Their walls were so thick they could withstand cannonballs. The castles were built to defend England against invasion from France or Spain. These countries were Catholic. Henry was worried that they would try to conquer England and make it Catholic again.

Hurst Castle in Hampshire was built by Henry VIII. It guards the entrance to the Solent – the stretch of water that leads to Portsmouth – where part of the Tudor English navy was based.

From arrows to muskets

In medieval times, archers won many victories using longbows. They helped Henry VII win the Wars of the Roses. The longbow continued alongside muskets at the beginning of the Tudor period. In 1595, however, Elizabeth replaced longbows with handguns.

HENRY THE KNIGHT

Lord Mountjoy wrote of Henry VIII: 'Our King is not after gold... but virtue, glory, immortality.' This tells us that Henry wanted to be a chivalrous knight.

In a tournament, knights wore full armour to protect themselves.

Ships and the navy

England is part of an island and has a long coastline. Tudor monarchs needed a strong navy to defend the country.

Fighting ships

Henry VIII built 59 fighting ships with heavy guns to fire at enemy ships. We know a lot about Henry's navy because one of his favourite ships, *The Mary Rose*, sank in 1545. The ship was raised from the sea bed in 1982. The guns and many things used by the sailors were still on board.

This statue of Sir Francis Drake stands on Plymouth Hoe. Drake returned here after he had sailed around the world.

Exploring the world

Elizabeth gave money to adventurers and sea captains to explore the world and open up trade routes. She did not object when they captured Spanish galleons laden with gold and treasure. Elizabeth used some of the gold to pay for more fighting ships.

This is a replica of the Golden Hind – *the ship Francis Drake sailed around the world. He set sail in 1577 and only returned three years later.*

The Spanish Armada

The attacks on Spanish ships enraged King Philip II of Spain. In 1588, he sent a large fleet of 130 ships, called an armada, to attack England. English ships fired on the ships as they sailed up the English Channel and then scattered them by sending burning ships among them.

SHIP WRECKS

Bad weather forced the Armada to return to Spain by sailing around north Scotland. Many ships were wrecked, and some still lie on the sea bed.

This is a model of an Armada ship. Large red crosses were painted onto the sails of the ships.

What does it tell us?

This **compass** was recovered from a wrecked Armada ship. It has a magnetic needle that points to the north. It floats on water so that it still works in rough seas. It shows that sea captains in Tudor times used instruments to navigate the oceans.

Royal splendour

Henry VIII and Elizabeth I used their wealth to impress foreign ambassadors and kings, as well as their own people.

Henry's palaces

Henry VIII had 55 palaces. The most impressive was Hampton Court. Henry used the palaces to entertain the **court** and foreign visitors.

Field of the Cloth of Gold

In 1520, Henry VIII and Francis I of France met near Calais in northern France to sign a pact of friendship. Each king tried to outdo the other with symbols of wealth and power. Francis erected a vast tent of gold brocade (woven material), while Henry built a brick palace filled with silk tapestries and carpets. The meeting place became known as the Field of the Cloth of Gold. There the two sides put on tournaments in which they jousted and wrestled each other.

The Tudor gateway to Hampton Court Palace is lined with rows of stone lions. Henry VIII spent a lot of money decorating and furnishing his palaces.

EXPENSIVE GUEST

It was so expensive to house Elizabeth and her court that some lords ran away when they heard she might come to stay!

Being seen

Elizabeth I was a popular queen, especially after her victory over the Spanish Armada. In return, Elizabeth loved her people and liked to appear in public. She took part in splendid processions. In summer, Elizabeth and the royal court travelled into the countryside on 'progresses'. These allowed country people to see her.

 A tapestry is a picture made of cloth that is hung on a wall. This beautiful tapestry is from the reign of Henry VIII.

What does it tell us?

This portrait of Elizabeth is called the Ditchley Portrait, because it was painted for Sir Henry Lee, a leading courtier who lived at Ditchley near Oxford. It shows the queen standing on a globe with her feet placed on England, showing her power over the whole country.

Entertainment

In Tudor times, people enjoyed themselves whenever they could.

Feasts and festivities

In most towns there were markets every week. As well as buying and selling goods, people met friends and drank ale in the local **tavern**. Travelling fairs toured the whole country. Paintings of these fairs show jugglers, dancing bears and other entertainment. Christmas celebrations lasted 12 days, during which the lord of the manor gave feasts for his friends and the local villagers.

Fun and games

People played games such as football and bowls. Henry VIII played an early form of tennis. Knights took part in tournaments. Young men were encouraged to practise their archery skills.

Families played musical instruments and board games such as backgammon or chess. Cards and dice were popular in taverns and at home.

Men and women enjoyed playing card games. The people in this painting are playing for money.

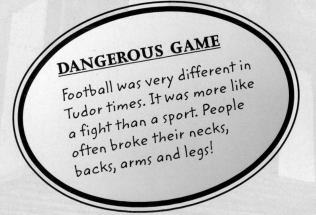

DANGEROUS GAME
Football was very different in Tudor times. It was more like a fight than a sport. People often broke their necks, backs, arms and legs!

Plays and players

Travelling actors, called players, toured from town to town. In London, several companies staged plays in specially built theatres. They hired actors and playwrights, the most famous of whom is Shakespeare. Elizabeth I enjoyed the theatre, and many plays were performed for her.

What does it tell us?

Shakespeare's Globe in London is an exact copy of the Globe Theatre of Tudor times. It shows us how Shakespeares's plays were performed. Wealthy audience members sat in the galleries. Poor people stood on the ground in front of the stage. They were called 'groundlings'.

Quiz

1. **Who was Henry VIII's first wife?**
    a. Anne Boleyn
    b. Catherine Howard
    c. Catherine of Aragon

2. **What was the Field of the Cloth of Gold?**
    a. A tapestry
    b. A large wheat field
    c. A place where Henry VIII and the king of France held a tournament

3. **Which of these were first used in Tudor times?**
    a. Four-poster beds
    b. Glass windows
    c. Lances

4. **What did most people drink in Tudor times?**
    a. Water
    b. Ale or mead
    c. Wine

5. **How often did most people in Tudor times bath?**
    a. Once a week
    b. Once a year
    c. Twice a year

6. **What job did William Shakespeare's father have?**
a. Glove-maker
b. Butcher
c. Teacher

7. **What is a musket?**
a. A horse-drawn carriage
b. A kind of gun
c. A musical instrument

8. **In which year did Francis Drake sail around the world?**
a. 1577
b. 1580
c. 1588

9. **Why did lords not want Elizabeth I to stay in their houses?**
a. She was too expensive to keep
b. Their houses were too small
c. She would never leave

10. **What did Elizabeth I like to do most?**
a. Hunt deer
b. Watch a play
c. Watch a football match

ANSWERS
6a
7b
8a
9c
10b

1c
2c
3b
4b
5c

Timeline

1485 Henry Tudor defeated Richard III at the Battle of Bosworth Field. This ended the Wars of the Roses. Henry was crowned Henry VII.

1509 Henry VII died and his son was crowned Henry VIII. Henry married Catherine of Aragon.

1516 Princess Mary was born.

1517 Martin Luther, a German priest, challenged the teachings of the Roman Catholic Church.

1520 Henry VIII and Francis I of France met at Field of the Cloth of Gold, near Calais, France.

1521 Henry wrote *The Defence of the Seven Sacraments*, for which the Pope gave him the title 'Defender of the Faith'.

1526 Henry VIII began to seek a divorce from Catherine of Aragon.

1533 Henry VIII married Anne Boleyn and Princess Elizabeth was born.

1534 Henry VIII became head of the Church in England.

1536 Dissolution of the Monasteries began.
Anne Boleyn was beheaded.
Henry VIII married Jane Seymour.

1537 Prince Edward was born, but Jane Seymour died.

1540 Henry VIII married and divorced Anne of Cleves.
Henry VIII then married Catherine Howard.

1542 Catherine Howard was beheaded.

1543 Henry VIII married Catherine Parr.

1545 *The Mary Rose*, one of Henry VIII's ships, sank off Portsmouth.

1547 Henry VIII died and his son was crowned Edward VI.

1553 Edward VI died aged 15 and his half-sister was crowned Mary I. She was the first woman to be crowned queen of England.

1558 Mary I died and her younger half-sister was crowned Elizabeth I.

1559 Elizabeth I was made head of the Church of England.

1577–80 France Drake sailed around the world in the *Golden Hind*.

1585 Sir Walter Raleigh set up Virginia, the first English colony in America.

1588 The Spanish Armada was defeated by the English navy.

1599 The Globe Theatre was built on the south bank of the River Thames.

1603 Elizabeth I died and the Tudor period came to an end.

Glossary

abbey A building where monks or nuns live.

ambassador A person sent by one country to represent them in another.

armour A metal or leather suit worn to protect the body in battle.

banquet A lavish meal or feast, often with many courses.

cannon A large gun that fires big, heavy balls made of metal or stone.

chivalrous Being brave, polite, helpful and honest — like an ideal knight.

christened To be given a name in a Christian ceremony called baptism.

compass An instrument that shows the direction of north.

court The king and queen with their advisors, servants and followers.

deeds A document that shows who owns a building.

ermine The white fur from an animal called a stoat.

joust A fight in a mock battle between two knights on horseback.

medieval The Middle Ages, which lasted from about AD 500 to about 1450

monastery A building where men called monks lived and worshipped God.

musket An early kind of handgun that came before the rifle.

parish register A church record of births, marriages and deaths.

Pope The head of the Roman Catholic Church.

population The total number of people living in a particular place.

Protestant A member of a Christian church that is not part of the Roman Catholic or Eastern churches.

Roman Catholic A member of the Christian church led by the Pope.

royal park A park or area of countryside owned by the king or queen.

rushes Dried grasses which are used like straw.

seal Hot wax with the owner's design pressed into it.

tavern A place, such as a pub, where alcoholic drinks are sold and drunk.

tutor A teacher who teaches children in their own homes.

voyage A long journey often made by ship.

woodcock A small bird that is caught and eaten.

Index

History from Objects

Contents of titles in the series:

The Egyptians

978 0 7502 6763 2

Who were the Egyptians?
Homes and towns
Farming and food
Clothes and crafts
Pharaohs
Pyramids and other tombs
Gods and temples
Mummies
The Egyptians at war
Writing
Quiz
Timeline

The Romans

978 0 7502 6762 5

Who were the Romans?
City of Rome
Roman town houses
The countryside
Food and drink
Clothes and crafts
Children and schools
Romans and religion
Defending Rome
Entertainment
Quiz
Timeline

The Victorians

978 0 7502 6764 9

Who were the Victorians?
The Industrial Revolution
Transport
The growth of cities
Houses and homes
Inventions and discoveries
Fashion and culture
Victorian families
Children - school or work?
Entertainment
Quiz
Timeline

The Greeks

978 0 7502 6767 0

Who were the Greeks?
City of Athens
Greek town houses
Farming and food
Clothes and crafts
Writing and myths
Children and schools
Gods and temples
The Greeks at war
Entertainment
Quiz
Timeline

The Tudors

978 0 7502 6765 6

Who were the Tudors?
The Tudors and religion
Tudor homes
Food and drink
Clothes
Children and schools
Castles and weapons
Ships and the navy
Royal splendour
Entertainment
Quiz
Timeline

The Vikings

978 0 7502 6766 3

Who were the Vikings?
Towns and homes
Farming and food
Clothes and crafts
Ships and travel
Warriors and raiders
Families and children
Gods and religion
Writing and sagas
Sports and games
Quiz
Timeline

WAYLAND